AF597998

BEACH GRASS

BEACH GRASS

Oliver Eldridge

C A N A A N

CONNECTICUT

1992

This book was set in the typeface Bembo by The Studley Press. The title page and dust jacket were set in Monotype Spectrum by M&H Type. The book was designed by Jonathon Nix, and printed by The Studley Press, Dalton, Massachusetts.

 Published by Oliver Eldridge, P.O. Box 1059, Canaan, CT 06018. Printed and bound in the United States of America.

ISBN: 0-9634194-0-4

Three pieces, *Drum Set*, *Holy Thursday*, and *Of Man and Moon*, previously appeared in *The Lakeville Journal* of Lakeville, Connecticut.

contents

FOREWORD

Fathers can be impossible . . . at times! This was the wrong time. As captain of the debating team of Drury High School I had expected to attend an evening rehearsal prior to next morning's debate at Williamstown High. To my dismay, however, after supper Dad told me that I was to accompany him that evening to Jessup Hall at Williams College, where Robert Frost was giving a public reading from his poetry. Obviously (to me) my responsibility was to participate in the rehearsal. I reasoned, pleaded, stormed in vain. As it turned out, that was the first of two debates that were lost!

Next day I lamely explained my absence to John Reilly, our debating coach and the head of the English department. Surprisingly he didn't seem upset, nor did he share my earlier exasperation.

That was the first, I think the best, of three public readings by Frost that I was to be privileged to hear. It is but rarely that writers perform public readings so clearly, so pleasingly, so effectively. My father had been right, but I doubt that I ever told him so. Teenagers!

Miss Mabel A. Tower of Drury's English faculty had introduced our sophomore class to analyses of contrived rhythm in verse—scanning for patterns of accent, determining the number of metrical "feet" in a line. We were trained to recognize figures of speech: simile, metaphor, personification, alliteration, onomatopoeia, and hyperbole. Later on we labored at precis writing, striving to condense a lengthy piece without loss of its essence, its force.

As juniors we were shocked upon our introduction to the free verse unorthodoxy of Whitman and Sandburg Perhaps by way of winning our acceptance, Miss Jessie

Sherman invited us to write a poem in free verse on a subject of our choosing. *Mount Williams* in this collection, slightly altered, was my attempt.

After a B.A. degree in economics from University of Maine and an M.A. in education from Boston University I, too, became an English teacher—first, at Arms Academy, Shelburne Falls, Massachusetts; next, at Drury in North Adams (my earlier alma mater) interrupted by wartime service in the navy; finally, at Housatonic Valley Regional High School, Falls Village, Connecticut. In 1957 I left teaching to work at Canaan Savings Bank, eventually serving as its president for eleven years. I retired in 1980.

When considering the possibility of producing a book of verse, I once thought it might be devoted to beekeeping, which accounts for a number of items on that subject here. Later I aspired to doing a collection of verses to be based on recent dazzling vistas in astronomy and space technology. Again, there are hints of this interest within these covers.

I am grateful for the encouragement of Alison Wyrley Birch and of fellow members of her workshop in creative writing for the past three years.

Louise, my wife, has shown continual interest in this project and, now, satisfaction in its conclusion. Her patience during long hours of my self-imposed isolation is recognized and appreciated.

Oliver Eldridge
P.O. Box 1059
Canaan, Connecticut 06018

May 4th, 1992

BEACH GRASS

Near where the sea in muted argument
Comes in soft crush upon the churning sand,
The beach grass bends before the element
Of air, inscribing circles on command.

Though myriad these grasses, each has space
Defined by sweep of its own borderline.
One blade—slim, limber—pivots at its base.
Its nutriment is thin and tastes of brine.

At the wind's whimsy, flexing to avert,
The grasses bow to buffets they forgive.
Each leaf-point swings in concert to assert
Its territorial imperative.

Each circumscribes the scope of its domain,
Encompasses ambition in a rune.
Drift wipes it out. It is inscribed again—
Delay the shifting, shaping of a dune.

The upright arc inscribes the level one
That driven sands repeatedly obscure,
But beach grass moves in wind—oblivion
Is held at bay as blade bends to endure.

DRUM SET

(An encomium to pandemonium)

Ditty-dom, ditty-dom, ching-ching BING!
One small boy on a big front porch—
Big front porch in the cool of an evening—
Cool evening cool, though a pulsing heat
Beats in the bent head, throbs in the feet.
Marvelous now how an orchestration
Builds with a flick-wrist syncopation,
Cymbal simmer and bass drum boom,
And rattle of snares as out of the gloom
March the heads-high Heroes of '76.
Now walking the rim are the talking sticks
With a stance, an advance, and a tap-dance prance.
There's a cow-bell clang and a touch that teases
As wire brush stirs with a rhythm that pleases
On a drumhead taut—then a gathering roll
That erupts in cacophonies to startle the soul
With a *bing-bang binky-bang BOOM-diddy BOOM*!

So the gloaming glooms as one small boy
Finds in his drum talk jubilance, joy.
There is free expression in this discussion,
And the points that are made are pure percussion.
In a big creation an occasional wonder
Are the smaller items that rattle and thunder.

A PIE SHELL IN THE CELLAR

In a box on a shelf in the cellar,
Done up in paper and twine,
Is stored a mourner's treasure—
A pie shell, its pattern fine
Pricked with a cooking fork once by one
Who had baked the shell, the underside
Of a pie unfinished, the day she died.
Then the relatives, sorrowing much,
Found the shell that had felt her touch,
Saw the old picture in humble dough
As they'd seen it hundreds of pies ago—
Arching branches of graceful tree,
And flowers, and birds—such artistry!
See the perfect flutings about the rim!
Tears will dry, and memories dim.
This knowing, they stored it cool and dry
So they could look at it bye-and-bye
For the image of her, whose dainty print
Had so glorified this household stint.
Thirty-two years they since have seen,
But the shell is dry, and whole, and clean.

Art is not only for palette and brush,
Or steel on stone, or tonal gush
Of wind past reed—for by broader creed
Many a master (mistress, too)
Of no matter how humble the tool—
Kitchen fork or carpenter's rule—
Has managed some beauty to impart,
Making homely labor, living art.

CELENDA

(In the margin of one page of an 1847 grammar, alongside conjugation of the verb *TO LOVE*, was found the penciled name *Celenda*—which suggests much.)

I have loved
Thou hast loved
He has loved Celenda

We have loved
Ye have loved
They have loved Celenda

Celenda sat four seats from him
And in another row.
Although his glance did stray to her,
He hoped she did not know.
He wrote her name in pencil next
The conjugation in his text.

I had loved
Thou hadst loved
He had loved Celenda

We had loved
Ye had loved
They had loved Celenda

Expression of past perfect love
Surviving, age to age,
Speaks without stammer, brings no blush—
Her name upon a page!

LOVE

You called me in the dark.
You called my name, I swear.
Conviction! Feet hit floor.
I stumble down the stair.

My light glows near your face
Composed in slumber sweet.
Serene, your even breath
But gently swells the sheet.

Now pounding heart can slow
As by your bed I stand.
All's well with you whose call
Will my response command.

TRAFFIC REPORT

Traffic is building on the interstate
And moving well when up ahead we spy
A snapping turtle—huge—initiate
A crossing, waddling slow with head held high.

We check the mirror, then accommodate
This fearsome dignity by changing lane.
Its rights to peaceful passage antedate
Those of us trespassers in its domain.

The turtle has supreme self-confidence
All else that moves, before it will give place.
Forward by instinct, not intelligence,
The clawed feet keep implacable their pace.

From the dark age of dragons it has come
With plated turret, massive jaws of dread—
State-of-the-art. We must admire the sum
Of time's technology from tail to head.

Six busy lanes it has to navigate
Proceeding fearlessly on primal quest.
From south to north it crawls at steady rate—
The eighteen-wheelers roaring east and west.

A tire may crush the sturdy carapace
Or nip it, flip it like a tiddly-wink
To travel a parabola through space,
Land in soft swale, to river-bottom sink.

This intersection has no sign nor light
Where Evolution, creeping toward destiny
Encounters Progress running day and night—
Its destination, Cleveland; schedule, tight!

ON NUMBER, SPACE, AND TIME

Infinity is quantity
Beyond imagining,
Number no lifetime can pronounce—
No eye's envisioning.

Out there one cannot add a one
Nor multiply by ten.
Digits and ciphers lose their powers
And use to mortal men.

The stars have their identities.
No snowflakes are the same.
Such individualities
Infinities proclaim.

Infinity can be reversed.
Far leftward slide the decimal.
Conversion by such sleight of hand
Makes things infinitesimal.

Infinity is lots of space—
No bottom, sides, nor top.
We haven't seen the end of it.
Out there it's hard to stop.

Arriving at infinity
I doubt I'd long abide,
For I have curiosity
To tour the other side.

On getting to infinity
I'd heave a mighty sigh,
Then would redo my measurement—
The distance verify.

Eternity is a dentist's chair
Or when a baby's crying,
Or when one has too much to do.
Too little, too, is trying.

Eternity, a long way off,
Is time in each direction:
The ultimate in what's ahead—
Or past. Your predilection!

Before the continents and seas,
Before THE BANG and shatter—
What darkness and what emptiness
Of energies and matter!

To contemplate eternity
Intrudes upon our time;
Consumed we more by day's concerns
Than reveries sublime.

A wise man said that what goes 'round
Comes around again.
I wonder if eternity
Ends where it did begin.

Beyond all heights, and widths, and depths
Is there a fourth dimension—
A vast expanse of timeless time
Beyond our comprehension?

Eternity . . . infinity . . .
Though one travel by express,
He still needs immortality
To get to each address.

We ask how many and how much
How far to go or come.
We can't abide forevers—
And must live by modicum.

NO WARMTH THERE IS IN MOONLIGHT

The scene is done in darknesses
Of shadow and of shade,
Awash in wan neutralities—
Impartial, still, and staid.

No warmth there is in moonlight.
Upstaging all the stars,
It lumines and it silhouettes
Without particulars.

But warmth there is in sunlight
To rouse us with its hail!
It comes with hallelujahs
Of color and detail.

Its greeting is a benison.
There's passion in its touch
To focus on some wrongs to right—
Supply is overmuch!

Light-of-moon is a hand-me-down
Sans ardor, fervor, zeal—
While light of sun, in line direct,
Both worth and work reveal.

"Give her a kiss from memory!"
"Give him a hug for me!"
Affection's warmth, like sunlight's,
Reflected can never be

STROKE AND RESCUE

At his door, a newspaper one day old
And milk bottles doffing their caps to cold
Give the alarm. Then we push inside
With a sense of fear that we do not hide.
Cold is this house! Are the fires out?
Henry McDougal just shuffles about,
Numbed and half-starved, and in disarray,
For his trousers were pulled on wrong today.
The pockets are not in their usual places.
Crossing his chest are backs of his braces.
A pipe, his comfort, adrift on the floor—
And nothing is now as it was before
When all went by schedule and neat design
With a wife's attention to time and line.
He speaks of warming up Sunday's stew
And surely senses some things to do,
But memory mixes with resolution,
Preventing accomplishment and solution.
Past days' repasts in inglorious link—
But good intent cluttering shelf and sink.
He stands in a world that is coming apart,
Once sweetly familiar now turned tart,
With things seeming seldom as they should be.
The woodwinds of winter in minor key
Moan at a corner, fret at a blind,
Mocking a man who is losing his mind.
Give tilt to the damper, shake to the grates!
Fling a shovel of coal—a defy to the fates!
Put fire to the kettle, knife to the bread.

A hot cup of tea, then get him to bed.
The thawed cricket chirps of his yesterdays,
Days of his horses, a team of matched grays
And talk of the crowds at Whitingham Fair.
Clear now his memory, taking us there.
Light now his laugh as he tells how it went—
Forty years gone since that happy event!

Spending its substance down the dark,
A meteor streaks to its final spark.
Consumed at the last to the stub of life,
Denied his function, deprived his wife,
McDougal is recued (though death be certain)
For a moment's glory before The Curtain.

HEARTBREAK, 1850

Three white marble stones, among many:

John A. Beckley	Sarah D. Wife of John A. Beckley
Died June 14, 1874 AE66	Died Sept. 17, 1850 AE 35

John
son of
John A. & Sarah D. Beckley
died Oct. 5, 1850
aged 4 Mos.

JOHN A. BECKLEY:

I buried my wife of thirty-five
While the world was green and our babe, alive.
I buried our babe when the world turned gold.
We had named him John. He was four months old.

Those were eighteen desperate days of life
Without his mother, without my wife—
Laid to her rest in the family lot.
Then, the bit-of-a-babe we had both begot.

I shall always miss her! Such dreary days
Without her laughter, without her praise!
And the little fellow of hope, our star—
Never learn to read, nor to travel far!

The bullfrog's chortle, the *konk-la-ree*
Of redwing perched in a marshland tree—
In such memories that had known her touch
She continues to live, for her loving much.

White marble gravestones I had prepared
For Sarah, for John, and for me—now spared.
In case she could know I did not forget,
Her favorite rose by her stone I set.

From our dooryard rose I had dug the shoot,
A thriving upstart from traveling root,
To favor the air with its scent in Junes
And gladden the eye with its gold doubloons.

Neighbors come calling—ask, how do you do?
And the days go by as the years will, too.
Her yellow rose as it grows will endeavor
To speak of my caring—now and forever.

TODAY'S GROUNDSKEEPER:

This job gets longer as the summers pass.
It seems that half my life I'm tending grass.
With riding-mower it is not too bad,
But when the day is over I am glad!

I used to know the people that I'd meet
At the post office, on the village street,
But now this has become the friendlier place.
I recognize a name, recall a face.

That tangled mess enclosed by iron rail
I shall remove tomorrow without fail.
The snarl of power-trimmer will resound
As I cut the prickly brambles to the ground.

Grass keeps me humping well into July.
For years I've seen this tangle, riding by,
But time for this tomorrow I can spare.
This lot has never had perpetual care.

OTTAVARIMAS

The dictionary Doctor Johnson wrote
A mean, disdainful humor did display.
When in the O's . . . for comment on the *Oat*,
Observing that in England oats and hay
Were provender for horses, he did note
In Scotland people ate the grain each day.
Meanwhile the English dined on Cheshire cheese,
Hot kidney pies, and Oriental teas.

Authorities in this enlightened age
Disparage Yorkshire puddings, cheese, and pies.
Now sirloin beef, the Briton's heritage,
And gravies thick—nutritionists despise.
Their edicts Samuel Johnson would enrage,
While oats, their grain of choice, the housewife buys.
If you would go at canter down life's course,
Eat like a doughty Scotsman . . . or his horse.

Note:
Ottavarima (Italian verse form, octave).

OCTOBER BEACH

Lambently illumined by the moon,
Dark cottages in line confront the sea,
Where heaving swells with spectral crests advance
To test a continent's solidity.
After long, murmuring mutters of retreat
Comes the crescendo of a comer's caving—
Then churning, shimmering, scurrying-up-the-beach,
The sideling sweep, siliceous froth, and laving.

The hour is late. We shiver in the chill.
Along the edge the salvos of percussion
Repeat the beat of rhythms in the night
As sea and shore continue their discussion.
They may their ancient differences work out.
Shore has been known for shifts in its position.
Sea, rising to occasions twice a day,
Will sometimes show a docile disposition—
But not tonight! There's thunder and there's thud
Of lace beneath the moon . . . and tossing scud.

WHITE SPIRE

The slender spire gleams white against the blue.
Here native builders fashioned from their wood
A steadfast beauty that they understood,
Simplicity and strength the Dorics knew.

This is a place of purity, not pride.
Here ministers have spoken words of power
To kindle goodly impulse. In the tower
The bell calls sabbath to the countryside.

The village, from the hill, is hid by trees
But for the spire. A spark of golden light
(The sun's reflected from this beacon's height)
Marks quiet haven from life's driving seas.

DISPUTE

Granite speaks: My name is Granite. Granite is my name.
I'll never change but ever be the same.
Braced and impacted like a wisdom tooth,
Consistent, hard, and tough—I stand for truth.
The wind is of no consequence to me,
For all that was, or is, must always be.
My purpose is to hold the world together
Just as I've done in every sort of weather.
On character my reputation clings
To bedrock basis in the scheme of things.

Wind responds: Wind is my name. You never find me home.
I travel at my whim. I love to roam.
I am a mischief-maker, quite the minx,
Strike up a dervish dance or scour the Sphinx
With desert sand and gravel till it blinks.
Flirtatious, fickle, impudent, profound—
I slam the door or roar an organ sound.
I like variety. I like to go,
To spin a duster, feel the vertigo.
I bring the snows that build a mile of ice
To grind the grit (millenia suffice)
That give a glacial facial not so gneiss.
Granite, if you could travel you would find
The beaches made of remnants of your kind.
You pride yourself on durability.
I find delight in instability.
Your hardness, Granite, doesn't much impress.
I'll stroke that jutting chin with my caress,
Flicking a fleck of matter as I go.

(You think it doesn't count and doesn't show!)
Woodland awakes to flutter, sway, and hum.
The grasses bow before me as I come—
Invisible, tempestuous, alive—
A passing presence, gone when I arrive.
The rain, the wave, the frost I bring with me
To wash, to slosh, to heave repeatedly,
Abrade the surfaces of the sublime
With substance of itself. I have the time.
I am the wind your character maligns—
Your perverse nurse checking your vital signs.

OF MAN AND MOON

Why do you want the moon?
Why tamper with the cosmic balances?
Be satisfied! Leave well alone!

Above your crib a ball swings, fascinating.

Born of past failure and borne high by Atlas-thrust
In decrescendo from the launching pad
Vaults the Agena. On to emptiness
So vast that speed seems insignificant,
To orbit briefly; then, on signal, flame—
Hurling Ranger off to rendezvous.

Cheers at Cape Kennedy and RCA.
Congratulations, too, at IBM,
Where known numbers of angels stand on heads of pins
And all are taught to THINK
In micro-waves and mega-distances,
Of random access digit computations,
Centrifugal, centripetal relations,
Of leads and drifts, rotations, revolutions.
Will Ranger televise from outer space
A face a quarter million miles away?
Will Ranger listen to your far command,
Recall your orders and perform your will,
Turn topsy-turvy in mid-course maneuver,
Put forth antennae, then extend its wings
Exposing silicon cells to solar power—
And speak distinctly down the distances?

The ancients went to Delphi for their answers,
And on matters for Diana's intervention
Journeyed to Ephesus, where the moon goddess' temple
Was one of seven wonders of the world.

Now questions quest and instant answers come—
A telemetric, electronic, parabolic,
Superb-ballistic miracle! Spin-spanning
To round rock imperturbably riding,
Potted by meteors, pitted, big as a barn,
Scarred by the eons' silent violence.
How sweet the moonlight sleeps on Pasadena
As this all-seeing Polyphemus moth
In split-tick strike digs Diana's hide—
Its shattered shards lost in Tranquility!

What impact has this fact upon your fancy?
How fare your necromantic lore? Romance?
Will you now wake from your Dark Ages dreaming,
Reach forth and touch the stuff of your illusion—
Or keep enchantment for a little while?

O, man—only a little lower than—
You plant potatoes at the dark of moon
And wait slack water at the moon's own time
Before sounding three blasts and easing Queen Mary
Back from her North River pier.
The loon laughs, and an October breathing
Ripples the golden of Lake Washinee.

THE OLD BARTON PLACE

At sugaring time when we gather a load
The team knows the turn at the Barton place road
And the stop as before where two maples stand
Like up-country couple of generous hand,
Still marking the dooryard—for husband, for wife.
They yield of their sweetness long after the life
Of those who first set them to grace their new home.
The house is a ruin, now silvery gray—
Its sills and its rooftree beset by decay;
Walls plastered and papered, now stained by the rain.
Don't walk on that floor—if you'd come here again!
The staircase ascends to a soft, evening sky;
It goes up, but the crumbly treads have gone by.
Come back in July to the field on the slope—
Now pasture of memory rather than hope—
Where knowing companion in quiet delight
Once parted the ferns to disclose to our sight
A spring walled in granite and up-to-the-rim
With heavenly water as sweet as a hymn.
The Barton place sleeps undisturbed by the rouse
Of farm boy in search of some wandering cows.
His thoughts are of Friday night's show in the town,
But not of the Barton place, so tumbledown.

LAND FEVER

(after Masefield)

O, take me back to the land again,
To land so firm and stable,
For chinaware when I breakfast there
Doesn't slide off the table.
I have had my day of cold, salt spray,
Of shuddering pitch and roll,
Of watches in rain that I must complain
Dampen and chill the soul.
Now what I require is a fireplace fire,
And a touch as soft as silk,
And blessings deep of a full night's sleep,
And a glass of beautiful milk.
So take me back to the land again,
To my most satisfactory wife.
I have had enough of the lonely seas
And enough of the sailor's life,
But instead of back to the land again
We are headed the other way
In a zigging, zagging convoy
Making fourteen knots, they say.
Our cargo? Admiralty oil
And Mustangs lashed topside.
We must heel and yaw forever
To deliver at The Clyde.

THE FIRST TIME I SAW SCOTLAND

The first time I saw Scotland we were steaming up The Clyde,
And I was sick of empty seas, rolling seas, wide.
The March day was breaking in a long, slow dawn.
Was it Scotland or fairyland I gazed out upon?
Aye, it was Scotland—and fairyland, too.
The hills swam in mist and the peaks swam in blue.
The sleepy little villages that curved along the shore
Appeared as though they'd been there for centuries before.
Once I stepped in Scotland I was in a storybook.
The Scottish folk were sturdy, had a scrubbed and ruddy look.
The bright gold of their daffodils—incomparably fair!
There was a certain element of magic in the air.
There were high, stone walls down a storybook lane,
The peanut-cart whistle of a fast Scots train,
The old lampposts of the lamplighter's time,
Little corner gardens—lovely as a chime,
Low-eaved cottages made out of stone
That English ivy had half overgrown,
And the extra touch of magic that is everywhere
When buds come green and spring is in the air.
No wonder bagpipe music has a wild and ancient cry!
It is singing in the Scottish peaks and ringing in the sky.
It is sight of hills like thunderheads that makes the kilties swirl
To the mad exhilaration that's the spirit of the skirl.
I must go back to Scotland in another day
To investigate the secrets of each loch and ben and bay,
To tramp among the Grampian Hills and watch cloud shadows race
Out and away from where I am, to some other place.
I shall have a pair of shoes made of Scotch-grain leather
Just to climb a crag or two and walk in the heather.

ONE DAY'S WONDER

While on a shaded, winding walk
Behind the Glasgow library
I saw two lassies deep in talk
Strolling just ahead of me.

The lassie with the violet eyes,
Whose age could scarce have been the sum
Of one hand's fingers, did apprize
My uniform and asked for gum.

Alas, my packs had not sufficed
Young Scotland's forays for one day!
Dismayed, I tore one stick across
And with it gave my last away.

The path went on into a dell
Of mystery, then to a height
Where Glasgow's university
Towered fair and bright.

Later I came to gardens where
Strange blossoms in profusion grew,
But the marvel of those violet eyes
Was the wonder that day knew.

EVENING AT ANCHOR, NORTH RIVER

The great water rises with the moon,
And the North River flows backward
Between the Palisades of Jersey
And glittering cliffs of the city.
The tanker, swung to meet the flow, is idle,
Its anchor lights bright over the dark.

Amidships the watch leans against the rail
While the moving legend of the amusement park
Spells itself over in endless tedium.
(The relief should come in forty-five minutes.)
Down river, the lighters, ferries, car floats, tugs
Are gliding gems—red, green, yellow—reflected.
To port, three hundred yards distant,
Riverside Drive sparkles with lights
Rocketing south, rocketing north—the clamor,
The strident screams for passage, now in different dimension.

That life, long known, its twinkling velocity
So simmering close, is one existence
Viewed by those from another, now knowing
The marvelous-tiered, blinking, glowing, sounding city
Is set on the brink of nights and silences
So many of its people know not.

TWILIGHT ON PURPLE ONE BEACH

Light on the high cloud fades. Dim grows the sea.
Ryukyu beach floats on tranquility.
An amph-trak still awash, in sand half-buried,
Rusted, and broken where its charge once carried
Men with the order to hit Purple One.
Four months ago it was—bazooka, gun,
Shrapnel, grenade, and bayonet moved on,
Their prize abandoned to oblivion.
Above the passive sea bellows no more
Once feared amphibian crawling at the shore.

FUJI

The mountain's snout once smoked malediction.
In the throat a convulsed incandescence
Reared and rolled in thunderous boil.
Strain surged against stress, brimming the crater's lip
As lava in white, squealing flood shot down.
Underground hammers shook the land.

Serene is the dawn off Yokohama.
In the west a white cone floats above cloud—
The flaring skirt of Fuji, a lady
Posed on the mists of morning.

TOKYO, 1946

Butterfly girls on the Ginza go
In bright, silk kimonos of long ago.
Wood shoes clopping in pace sedate,
In time they come to a great, stone gate
By water below them, dark as night
And chatter in pleasure at sudden sight
Of scarlet carp in the palace moat
And waterlilies abloom, afloat.

Then clop, clop, clopping they make their way
Up a bridge to the grounds of the Son of Day,
Where they stop in line—and paragon
Are their bows to the Emperor of Nippon.

SURVIVOR

OOS-la . . . oos-la . . . oos-la . . . oos-la;
OOS-la . . . oos-la . . . oos-la . . . oos-la—

THE BEAST between shafts of a two-wheeled, open cart
IS A MAN drawing uphill—steadily . . . so slowly . . .
A load of corrugated roofing—rusted, bent.
The sun is hot. Wooden hubs creak. He gasps

OOS-la . . . oos-la . . . oos-la . . . oos-la—

THE MAN between shafts of a two-wheeled, open cart
IS A BEAST of resolute heart—though an old one, a sad one—
Who salvaged these scraps of yesterday's Yokohama
Lying ignored since nights of incendiaries—
Magnesium, phosphorus—showered the flammable city
To cries of alarm, dismay; of terror, disorder—
Everywhere blazing, smoking; blowing embers, ash.
Today he moves by metronome chant, by one-step surges—
Brow-band taut, back bent toward the road's rising.

OOS-la . . . oos-la . . . oos-la . . . oos-la . . .

THE MAN IS A MAN in the shafts of an open cart,
Enduring the wearying work, the drag of the load
For worth to be found in the ash of disaster,
And means, in twisted pieces of despair,
And purpose—to flatten these random remains, to establish
Some new unity against the certainties
Of rains, of winds, of cold.

A LIGHT SKIRMISH DURING A LONG WAR

For weeks had our ship been awaiting new orders.
We were anchored at Malakal, just off Koror.
Weary of heat and monotonous watches,
The crew wanted home, near the end of the war.

With not much to look at, too little to do—
At a place never heard of and better forgot—
We were hooked to a bottom and chained at the bow
And would rot out our days in this sweltering spot.

Our luck seemed to turn when the captain discovered
A binocular heaven but three miles away.
An island of palms, with a small dock for mooring,
Could be used for a two-hour liberty stay.

By the time they arrived in their open-air boats
The off-watch had been broiled by the tropical sun.
Disembarking, they headed for shade of the palms.
Finding something to drink was priority one!

No greeter was there with a glass or a cup,
No hut habitation, commercial concession,
But hundreds of coconuts lay strewn about.
Could milk of the coconuts quench their obsession?

First, get off the husk to the nut if you can!
The sailors assaulting, determined, persist
By bouncing them, prying, and poking with knives.
Though battered by boulders, the husks all resist.

At last frustrated, flustered, sweating, and hot,
The navy was tiring, admitting defeat
When a slip-of-a-girl, dark of skin and of hair,
Like an angel appeared to help men-of-the-fleet.

She picked up a coconut, walked through the crowd
To four feet of pipe sticking out of the ground,
Scraped the coconut cheek on the edge of the pipe
While shredding off husk—to a silence profound!

Now down to the nut! At a blow with a rock
Its brittle shell cracked, then was split with a blade.
One man took a mouthful . . . then spewed it all out!
We laughed at the ghastly grimace that he made.

Back at the dock we found one boat half-flooded—
Submerged at the bow, with the stern in the air.
Some holiday sailor had used too short a line.
Then the tide had come in. What a sorry affair!

Baffled by coconuts, outdone by a girl,
And flunking in seamanship—just off Koror—
Our liberty party returned to monotony
From a tropical isle, near the end of the war.

AROUND ABOUT A MIRROR

Bright waters pour in crystal-cold cascade—
Tumultuous, in tortuous descent
To quiet places where the herons wade,
Attentive in their search for fingerlings.
The ancient pine by trunk and branch extends
Its horizontal reach across the flows—
By cramped progression, convoluted twist
Past weathered stub, and gnarl, and knob, and knurl
To evergreen in archipelagoes.
A brown-robed monk, his arms behind him, views
The Eastern temple with the two-tiered roof,
Its corners upswept like the prows of ships.
O, such a day of pastel butterflies,
Of varied shrub and tree florescences—
Soft shades of blue, and white, and apricot—
While on precarious perch a songbird swings!
Down in the vale the now meandering stream
Is bridged by arch of stone from Here to There.
Above its wall, the figure of a man
Wheeling a pushcart, its umbrella furled,
Intrudes ambition in a realm of gold.

MOUNT WILLIAMS

Northern bulwark of the Greylock Range,
There in perfect contour you stand aloof—
Buffeter of storms, mad trysting place of winds,
Like a god you stand, withdrawn.
Thoughts pass hourly across your face—
Never the same thought.
I have seen you at dawn in mid-winter
When the air was fine, and new snow thick, and
the dawn rosy,
And your crystal top in rosy reflection sparkled—
An intangible dream, a faerie domain.
"Heaven!" I breathe, but way up there
It is cold—terribly cold—and lonely.
And I have seen you in spring wrapped in verdure.
And I have seen you somnolent in summer sunshine.
And I have seen you in red riot in autumn.
And I have seen you brooding on a dark day.
And I have seen you standing wet and disheartened
in the rain.
And I have seen you after the rain higher and mightier
than ever.
You are purity. You are majesty. You are patience.
You are a bulwark of the Greylock Range.
Vainly I climb to your summit—
I have not conquered you; I cannot conquer you,
For you are purity . . . majesty . . . patience.
Like a god you stand, withdrawn

THE ALCHEMIST

(Vladimir Horowitz—Moscow, 1986)

Acknowledging applause that greets him now
From half a life and half a world away,
The aged expatriate fulfills their dream—
That in this hall and in another day
Nobility, and loveliness, and praise
Transformed to music would their spirits raise.

First, at the keyboard his deft fingers dwell
In reverie, in memory awhile,
Then nimbly run to phrasing intricate,
Repeated patterns done with ease and style.
They blithely go a-dancing on their toes
Or manly march to great fortissimos.

Complexities of repertoire recalled,
Diverging and converging harmonies
In descants, counterpoint, arpeggios
To rise or tumble to their destinies—
Cascading cadences at his control
That animate and fortify the soul.

Such music no composer can express
By scribing clefs and dots upon a page,
Nor student emulate by discipline,
By his inert fidelity engage.
The master is embarked upon the sea;
His craft responds with spontaneity.

Like gem illumined on dark silences
The simple phrase or single note is set.
By shifting shadings, symmetries adrift
Remembrances and moods again are met,
Reflections and affections lingering
Upon the fancy of his fingering.

Conspiracies clandestine are forgot.
Years of deception, bitterness, and fears,
For love allays suspicion and distrust.
Joy blooms on faces somehow streaked by tears.
Affinity and insight glorify
Familiar *Polonaise* and *Traumerei.*

With fire the alchemist performs the rite
Of interplay on keys of black and white,
And ebony and ivory transmutes
To colors glorious by his attributes.

SHADES OF SPRING

A world of color, this!—its light and shade
In glorious interplay of mien and mood.
The shades of spring are in the spectrum laid
By vernal equinox from March to June.
The hues into each other blend and fade
From misty element to darker jade.
The first is but an optimistic hint;
What follows comes in ever stronger tint,
As from shy essay to full-blown success—
From that we see not but can vaguely feel
To that we see full well and feel no less.

It starts with work of frost and thaw,
And slosh of sap, and raucous caw
Of crows in darkness of the pines.
Follow the sledge and find the signs
Of rabbit and fox where they crossed the road.
Horses steam as they drag the load,
And water winks in the runner tracks
In the mud. A word, and the creaking slacks.
The team stands patient. The gatherer goes
Up over his knees in drifted snows.
Into his shining pail is poured
A flood of last summer's sunlight stored.

In emptied bucket a plaintive *ting*
As fresh drops come to fill the thing.
The gatherer calls. The team moves on
To curve in the road where the man has gone.
Sap foams into the tank and then

They are off down County Road again.
In the sugarhouse by mountain stream
Are the roaring arch and pan with steam
Rôlling upward and out of sight—
Fog by day and cloud by night.
This is the scene of the boiling down
Of sap to syrup golden brown.
Arch doors glow in a cherry red
From heat within. Behind, the shed
Stacked with slabs of hemlock and oak
Whose destiny's flame, and spark, and smoke.
Tending the gates of the bubbling pan—
And heart of the enterprise—a man,
The hardy farmer who distills
Some of the sweetness of these hills.

Days slip by. The color grows
From hint to hue. In woods the snows
Like shadows lie behind rock and hill.
Comes flash of blue on a morning chill!
In broken orchard the chortling glee
Of robin telling of things to be.

Through last fall's leaves runs the lacy line
Of that elfin miracle, princess pine.
Arbutus bloom will the season greet—
Never was ever a fresher sweet!
A horse, long weary of pull and plod,
Rolls in delight on the drying sod.

From under a street light branches are bars,
And new buds dance in the night like stars.

By day the display is of dainty drops
Of pastel elegance in the tops
That the slow sun warms to revived belief
That spring *is* here—with lilac leaf
Grown to the size of a mouse's ear.
How green the grass! And skies, how clear!

Green is the year. With a sudden run
Buds become leaves shaking hands with sun.
Under fruit trees so recently skeleton bone
Petals are sprinkled that wind has strown.
White lilacs, purple—nod in the weather
Like plumes on knights riding off together.
From green to greener the shadings blend
As spring's fresh glories its old transcend,
And long light hints of the season's end.

PROCESSION OF CLOUDS

Fair winds prevail. Flotillas cross the blue
From yon to whither—marshalled, in array.
The splendid galleons pass as in review;
Each, lightsome gossamer and silver gray.
Formed and reformed, pliant before the blow,
Visible vapors that thin air gave birth
Proceed in majesty their onward flow
Beyond their meeting with the rim of earth.
No need for trumpets, nor calliope,
Nor base drum thumping beat as they depart.
Silent they move in blessed tranquility.
Silent they move together, though apart.

CAN THAT BE THUNDER?

Rouse from your slumber to a flicker-flit—
Heat lightning probably—and far away.
Then rouse again to muffled cannonade—
Perhaps too far to reach us, though it may.

Count out the seconds from the flash to boom
That makes the windows rattle in respect.
Divide by five to calculate the miles
From source of the commotion, in effect.

Must be up north another town or two—
The answer comforts while in bed you lie,
But soon there's sizzle-snap with greenish flare
And BANG. You're on your feet. The curtains fly!

Scramble and scurry. Lowering of sash.
The sills are wet. Wind beats against the pane.
There's crash and rumble-tumble overhead—
Bombardment that big thunder guns maintain.

The scene is lit by momentary blitz
Then plunged anew in dark disharmony.
The cymbals clash. The kettledrums intone
Ill-tempered energy in tympany.

Thor throws his hammer randomly about.
Valkyrie winds ride with the rush of rain.
High drama this, equipped with thunder-sheet
Off in the wings, to sound of doom again.

Fury and sound are making their retreat.
Harmless, they seem, and signifying naught.
The spectacle enlivening a night
Was tantrum merely, sultry days had brought.

In time the surly grumble will subside,
The old leak stop its dripping in the pail,
But shattered trunk may block a busy street—
Or good friends lose their home, as sirens wail.

BEACH BOTTLE

A corked whiskey bottle stuck its neck and one shoulder
Out of the sand somewhere north of Miami—
Its barnacles evidence certain
It had been all-at-sea even longer than I.

How good it must feel to be back in safe hands!
I thought and eagerly scanned the interior
Hoping some sailor had unburdened a part of his soul
And set it adrift to me.

Alas! He would not commit it to writing
(Or else he had nothing to say)
But had set the cork in a whiskier whimsy
For a vacuous voyage
Among unsteady breaths and eddies of the world.

FLY-OVER

How these honky-tonk geese, like a V in the sky,
Give a lift to the heart, a delight to the eye!
With a gabble of talk the formation sweeps by
In discourse on their course, or the height that they fly,
Or the laggard-in-line that has made it awry . . .
And we hark to their bark . . . as it tries to comply.

Just above the horizon! We barely descry
But their light, penciled mark, catch the whisper of cry.
They are gone in the morning they so glorify.
They are lost in the mist. We awake with a sigh.

LEAF STORM

On this dark day of glorious hurrahs,
Of wild dispersal of a school let out,
There is a storm of leaves abandoning,
Caught-up in eddies, tossed, and sailing far—
Bright coins by Fortune lavished to the blow.
The flecks and flickers scintillate and swirl
In spiral frenzy as they race about.
These are the end-of-season castaways
Defying all the gravities of life—
Discipline, order, purpose—to the winds
To celebrate inebriate holiday.
With tumbling chitter-chatter on the walk
And scratchy skitter-scatter on the road
They fly all helter-skelter to the sky.
One gust propels a charge to save the day.
A teapot tempest turns to whirligig.
It seems we are immersed in merriment.
It lights upon the head; it strokes the cheek.
Some throaty gusts bespeak a coming rain
To dampen-down this dancing in the street,
This random ramble-scramble everywhere
To fill the hollows, spin into the lees
Of fences, walls, and corners—bedding down
In dunes and drifts, a mix of crimson, gold.
Crimped edges interlock—arthritic grips—
Denying prying fingers of the wind.
Rain comes, perhaps an early spate of sleet.
Sodden, they settle. Scarlet, orange, gold
Fading to amber, umber underfoot—
A mishmash come from myriad family trees.

A generation gone! A pageantry!
We would run-through it all another time
And consecrate a day to spectacle . . .
To listen and to watch, another year.

ALBANY MARKET

The banked fire slumbers in the stove all night
As cold creeps in at crack beneath the door
And rimes the keyhole with a rim of white
To chill the dark interior of the store.

Hooked to a wire, bananas hang by hands—
Black silhouettes upon show window gloom.
Pale cabbages await the trade's commands—
Dim, crescent moons that street lamps scarce illume.

The marshaled lines and files, as for review,
Proprietor now sleeping did ordain.
From lettuce, carrot, grapefruit, honeydew
Vapors congeal to crystal on the pane.

A key turns in the lock to start the day.
Boots stomp off snow, and mittens chafe the cheeks.
A wrench shakes down the ash without delay.
A poker nudges coals. The damper squeaks.

Contriving phalanxes and pyramids and strings
Of braided onions is greengrocer art.
He prides himself on his accomplishings
In which his wife Francesca plays a part.

He notes the window frosted up again.
Then gives attention to the things to do.
It happens on cold mornings now-and-then.
The produce on display will not show through.

Behold the scene! Translucent, silver-gray,
In frozen fresco from Triassic time
Long fronds of undersea ascend and sway,
And vines arise; their tendrils coil and climb.

Transpiring essences new forms assume,
The ghosts of leafage, done by overlay—
The blade, the fiddlehead, the graceful plume—
It is reincarnation in a way.

The sun is up! The silver, shot with gold
That flecks the crystal tinsel stretched on high.
It sparks the barbs on brambles of the cold
And random rocket-bursts that light a sky.

The stove, the sun work to a common end
And spoil the spectacle of the display.
A rivulet of tear starts to descend
The cheek of winter. So begins the day.

PANDORA'S BOX

The express truck stopped outside our door.
The man alighted, strolled 'round to the rear.
He lifted out a package and set it on the floor
Gingerly, his valor mixed, of course, with fear.
Not that I blamed him! What a fearsome hum!
From Georgia these three pounds of bees had come.
Beneath the steady roar we, listening,
Heard claws ticking the wire screen and saw
The golden underbodies glistening.
Here marvelous capacities were caged
While they with frantic wings their protests raged.
Pandora sure must have her veil about
The moment that these vagrants are let out!

The expressman grinned and touched his hat.
"Five eight five—collect," he said,
Took bills and silver, then he fled
Relieved that that was that.

FRUIT BLOOM

Fly, honeybee, fly!
Winesap, Baldwin, McIntosh, Spy—
Sprays of bloom on a bright, blue sky.
Sun is warm. Air is light.
Half the world is white, white, white.
Fly, honeybee, fly!

Work, honeybee, work!
Air is light. Blossoms hum
With honey-flow delirium,
For sun is warm. The month is May—
So back to the hive without delay.
Work, honeybee, work!

SWARM

Noon in the bee yard as a calliope
Plays one long note, a high hum, sustained—
Sound of creation saying *yes*.
The whirling cosmos, the slow-spinning nebula
Begins to move through space.

When it is gone we are back on Main Street;
The circus has just gone by.

BEE A-BORNING

Here in the city of cradles the throng mingles—
Each bee intent on its own work,
Each intent on the work of all.
A porous dome is rent by a crescent cut.
A capping swings outward on its hinge.
Revealed, the face immutable—
Black antennae lifting
And black, compound eyes.

Rest.

Slow, slow extrication:
Head . . . thorax . . . abdomen.
Then, mobile, free,
Tremulous, hesitant,
Pale and unsteady . . .
With wisdom of ages,
Law of commonwealth mastered—
In birth unheralded, uncelebrated—
One new bee merges with the throng
And brushes the strangeness off its down.

WINGING IN

(After John Masefield's *Cargoes*)

Out of the sun, their trajectories interweaving,
Come the golden bullets when their flight is spent.
They drop upon the entrance board, touch-talk with others leaving
On matters of deflection, range . . . and maybe armament.

Out of the blue, on various tacks and reaches
Come heavy-laden galleons from the far-away isles—
Islands of goldenrod and purple aster beaches
Where the soft breeze washes and the sunlight smiles.

Up to the busy countinghouse, whose specialty is import,
Come waddling Dutch burghers with bulging pantaloons.
With such wealth as they must carry they are not apt to tarry
And scarcely take the time to say good afternoons.

LINING BEES

Alton invited, "Come if you please!
I am off for the morning, lining bees."
Goldenrod gold was the field, in effect
Answer divine to some man's neglect.
He set the small box on an upright stick.
His cupped hands caught a bee, with motion quick
Popped it inside where it buzzed in vain
Its confined fury on small, glass pane.
Soon anise and syrup changed its mind;
It settled to gorge upon its find.
Slipping the glass, and with flour paste
Alton dabbed its thorax white in haste.
A minute more and the bee took wing,
Circled and circled to fix the thing
On its chart by bearings. Then blazing light
Dazzled. We lost the line of flight.
The hours were happy as long as we stood
In the humming field, though try as we would
No line established from box to tree.
Both southward and northward it might have run,
And circling bees would be lost in the sun.

It was years ago that we vainly lined
Bees to a bee tree we could not find.
If reached it might have been dearly bought.
Its sweetness lay mostly in the thought.

THE FALLING FROM GRACE OF THE DRONES

The drones are a party
With appetites hearty
But no disposition for gain.
They've a swaggering swing
When aloft on the wing
But from labor they ever abstain.

The drones are a faction
Inured to inaction
Whenever the weather looks grim.
They are sunshine disporters
With government quarters,
Though their lives are but matters of whim.

With chill of September
Their sisters remember
And sweet of the comb they withhold.
Then harassed, afflicted,
The drones are evicted
To perish outside in the cold.

They are portly patricians
Without inhibitions.
They roister, and slumber, and dine—
But when summer is done
Early frosts are the Hun,
And their fall is a Roman decline.

HONEY HARVEST

Girded for battle, shoulder to shoulder,
The Amazons wait in solid phalanxes
To repel the assault imminent
On the City of Gold.

Puffs of white smoke eddy over the barbicans.
The martial array melts in disorder, and the Amazons
Find other matters more pressing—in strange disbelief
That fire and pillage sometimes work together.

WHAT HONEY, THIS?

What honey, this?
We hardly know—
Unless the honey
Of touch-and-go.

Flavor? Not clover
Nor goldenrod flow,
But blend of all blossoms
That bees touch and go.

It was *touch* to gather
And *go* to keep
With hope for enough
When snows lie deep.

COMB HONEY

Common man may dine in state—
Square of honey on a plate—
With silver knife to cut a chip.
He watches golden fragrance drip.

Crumbling castles of the bee
Ooze the work of alchemy.

Let it run upon the tongue.
It is the sweet of summer sun.
It is the wine of summer wind.
It is the lifting of the wing.

SILENT CITIES

A cold sky lowers. Beyond the fence
Are spruces stirring in their tents.
Across an open space winds blow
Small eddies on the crusted snow.
The hives sleep quiet for the night
Beneath their blanket deep and white.
With scarce the stirring of a wing
The silent cities dream of spring.

CELEBRATION

Come, celebrate the sun-spun mists of earth,
All sensible to glory in the worth
Of hard hills softening to golden greens,
To reds, to browns of budding—pleasant scenes
Of constellations shining in a lawn,
Of birdcalls chorusing at dawn: *Rebirth! Rebirth!*
Come, celebrate these sounds of spring again—
Yes, the beatitude of quiet rain;
Too, the commandment swelling root and grain—
The melody, the mystery, the mirth!

REFRACTIONS

The sun before me was blinding bright
As I crossed a lawn that the airs of night
Condensing had spangled with gleaming drops.
It was more than water that wet my shoes—
But fire of diamonds—greens, golds, blues!

The brilliance of truth too strong to face
Refracted shines from the commonplace.
Quick glance at the sun will the eyes subdue
That would linger on bronze in a glint of dew.

TO A WANDERING AIR

Miss Indecision, where now will you go—
To give day-lily trumpets a tentative blow?
Or to watch pasture birches bow graceful adieu
As you veer toward the hills that are far-away blue?

Mistress Meander, say—whither away—
To set cottonwood leaves in a quivering play?
To ripple through meadow? Put smiles on a river?
Or send a girl running indoors all a-shiver?

The whimsical ways of a wandering air
Send it gleefully forward; its prospects seem fair,
So it quickens its stride. Then contrarily
Drops to rest . . . catch its breath . . .
momentarily.

SN'S

First, one's temper gets SNippy; he starts in to SNiff
As he dabs at his SNoot with a big handkerchief.
Then a shiver of chill brings a frenzy of SNeezes,
And he SNuffles and SNorts in a way that displeases.
An old Down East treatment for cold-in-the-head
Is to SNuff salt-and-water and march off to bed.
Soon, SNoozing and SNoring, he finds in repose
Relief from annoyance at end of his nose.

ON KATAHDIN ONE NIGHT IN OCTOBER

At dusk as Chimney Pond Camp we neared,
The snowing stopped, and the cold air cleared,
And we stared at ice on the mountain wall
And frozen form of a waterfall.
The sky was pale and the mountain gray
As we stomped into the cabin to stay.
We made the acquaintance of four inside
And warmed our supper while Dudley, the guide,
Told mountain lore of tall-tale brew—
But he made it alive, and his voice rang true!
Then his stories were lost in the crashing roar
Of wind that battered at roof and door.
Frying pans hanging on nails on the wall
Clattered and clanged to the rise and fall
Of eddying air (though the logs were chinked)
And their burnished backs in the lamplight blinked.
The cabin shuddered while wind at work,
Blocked by wall of the glacial cirque,
Strove by all the force it could muster
To blast us out of that place of bluster.
Chilled in the room where the stove glowed red,
Beneath nine blankets we went to bed.
Our fingers shook as they put out the light;
We shivered that riotous winter night.

BOAT PEOPLE

Drifting for weeks on a sea of forgetfulness,
Pitching and rolling for ever so long,
Ragged, bedraggled, ignored in their hopelessness
By masters of shipping en route to Hong Kong.

Hungry or fevered, ensnared in barbed wire,
Wary of promises, sick of delay,
To be far from the terrors of home—their desire.
Edicts of governments bring them dismay.

Molested, neglected, they call from their pen,
Scum of humanity no one wants in.
All look alike to the government men
Blind to the talent and purpose within.

CATHEDRAL PINES

(Cornwall, 1989)

I.

Sacred this hillside was. Hemlock and pine
Dimmed the day's glare as in a holy room.
A place of heaven-on-earth, it seemed, these woods.
Two hundred fifty years—since settlement—
They were preserved. No rasping drone of saw,
No axe, no peavey, drag-chain, straining team
Belittled the magnificence of these.
Before majestic Presence one in awe
Stood in this temple. Columns beyond count
Soared upward. Needled architraves of boughs
Filtered the sun to the dun duff below,
Where roots invaded crevices in ledge
And cracks in granite, questing after damp.
With such firm bases and such pedestals
These pillars seemed forever in their strength—
A thousand seasons proving: they endure.

II.

Come, see the devastation for yourself—
The prostrate tangle of great, tapered shafts,
Their roots uprearing, branches rent and gone.
The eye sees little else. It's on and on,
Destruction on a scale as would suggest
A meteor impact or the grinding slip
Of earth's tectonic plates. But this was air—

The stuff of zephyrs, wafter of fragrances!
Along a front two masses did contend,
Set up a swirl, a counterclockwise spin,
A cyclotron. Its compressed energy
Assaulting objects perpendicular
To send them sailing, tear them, bring them down.
The thunderous thud of falling, cracking, rush—
All protest drowned in elemental roar,
Lost in the bellow of this monstrous rout.
No letup in the torment, no reprieve.

III.

"It's God's will," someone says, attributing
A purpose quite beyond our need to know
To Deity—and also to imply
A trust: whatever tragedy befall,
The worst event will work to some good end
Eventually, if not in our own time.
This was an Act of God, beyond control—
So pick up after Him as best you can.

Such thinking troubles others who maintain
No God of their believing would so strike
The upright, bringing aspirations down
In wild confusion, wasting, and dismay.
When what is straight and right seems targeted,
What circumstance evokes response like this?
Their God, involved with myriad concerns
In this galactic system and the next,
Upon occasion, late to intervene,
Becomes a grieving God when things go smash.

HOLY THURSDAY

Mine are the eyes that will not watch.
My lips the friendless Lord deny.
This is the fist that buffets Him.
I join the call to crucify.

Firmly conforming to *Pax Romana*
Ever I do not what I know.
The cross swings stark against the sky
In a present moment of long ago.

A nail am I in wincing flesh,
The pressing, blooded point of thorn,
A sponge of vinegar on a reed
Thrust in spite at a face forlorn.

O, wonder not at the shaking earth
Or veil of the holy temple split—
Wonder not at the hours of dark,
For woe it is to think of it!

Lost at sea on an ice floe breaking,
Trapped down the corridor of a mine,
I yearn for pardon unearned, sustaining—
Long for a glimmer from light divine.